Norwood House Press
PO Box 316598
Chicago, Illinois 60631

For information regarding Norwood House Press, please visit our website at:
www.norwoodhousepress.com or call 866-565-2900.

Photo credits:
Library of Congress (4, 10, 11, 12, 17, 18, 23); American International Pictures (19);
Associated Press (21, 28, 29, 30, 34, 35, 38, 39, 41);
Ronald Reagan Presidential Library (22); LBJ Presidential Library (44).

Cover Photos: AP Photo/Julie Jacobson (left), Getty Images/Spencer Platt (right)

Edited by Mark Stewart and Mike Kennedy.
Designed by Ron Jaffe.
Special thanks to Content Consultant Kim Greene.

Library of Congress Cataloging-in-Publication Data

Harrison, Geoffrey.
  Lethal weapons / by Geoffrey C. Harrison and Thomas F. Scott ; edited by Mark
Stewart and Mike Kennedy.
      pages cm. -- (Great debates)
  Includes bibliographical references and index.
  Summary: "Informational text uses a historical framework to discuss issues
surrounding gun rights and gun control. Sections include opinions from
notable Americans on various sides of the issue followed by encouragement
for readers to analyze each opinion."— Provided by the publisher.
  ISBN 978-1-59953-592-0 (library edition : alk. paper) --
  ISBN 978-1-60357-572-0 (ebook)
1. Gun control--United States--Juvenile literature. 2. Firearms
ownership--United States--Juvenile literature. I. Scott, Thomas F. II.
Title.
  HV7436.H374 2013
  363.330973--dc23
                          2013014298

COVER: Guns have always had a place in American society, but some
believe that our culture would be safer with certain controls of firearms.

GREAT DEBATES

TOUGH QUESTIONS / SMART HISTORY

LETHAL WEAPONS

By
Geoffrey C. Harrison
and
Thomas F. Scott

NORWOODHOUSE PRESS

CHICAGO, ILLINOIS

Contents

INTRODUCTION

Note: Words that are **bolded** in the text are defined in the glossary.

INTRODUCTION

Pub. for the Proprietors by R.H.Hobson. Chesnut St Philad.ª 1829.

THE NATIONS BULWARK.

We have issues ...

History doesn't just happen. It isn't made simply with the delivery of a speech or the stroke of a pen. If you look closely at every important event in the story of America, you are likely to discover deep thinking, courageous action, powerful emotion ... and great debates.

This book explores the ongoing debate about gun rights in the United States. It looks at an issue that, for many, boils down to what it actually means to be an American. Some of the arguments you read about in this book will be familiar— people have been making them for more than a century. Other issues are more recent.

The issue of gun control in the U.S. actually has its roots in 17th century England. King James II was Catholic and tried to take guns away from Protestants. After James abandoned the throne, all Englishmen demanded—and got—a Bill of Rights that guaranteed the right to bear arms.

This sketch from the 1800s pokes fun at the Philadelphia militia. The need to form a "well regulated militia" is at the heart of the gun rights debate.

Join the Debate

Debate is the art of discussing a controversial topic using logic and reason. One side takes the affirmative side of an issue and the other takes the negative side. Remember, however, that a great debate does not necessarily need to be an argument—often it is a matter of opinion, with each side supporting its viewpoint with facts. The key is to gather enough information to create a strong opinion. Out in the real world, debate has fewer rules and can get noisy and ugly. But on the big issues in America, debate is often how compromises are made and things get done.

These struggles were on the minds of the English settlers who colonized America during the 1700s. Each colony had its own constitution, and most included the right of individuals to own and use guns. Colonists needed firearms for hunting and protection. Many were skilled marksmen.

When the founding fathers began writing the Constitution, James Madison was asked to spell out the right to bear arms in the Second Amendment. The final version reads: *A well regulated **militia** being necessary to the security of a free state, the right of the people to keep and bear arms shall not be infringed.*

Madison's use of the word "infringed" made it clear that the right to own guns should not be limited. Some people claim the debate over gun control begins and ends with this distinction. Others believe that Madison linked gun ownership to national security. At the time, there was a

Make Your Case

In Chapter 2 through Chapter 5, you will find special sections entitled **Make Your Case**. Each one highlights different sides of the debate on gun rights using quotes from prominent Americans. **Make Your Case** lets you analyze the speaker's point of view … and challenges you to form an opinion of your own. You'll find additional famous opinion-makers on the gun rights debate in Chapter 7.

threat that the English (or another foreign power) would attack the United States.

The founding fathers could not foresee the changes that would take place in America in the centuries that followed. That was a major reason why they created the Supreme Court, which makes the final decision when the Constitution needs clarification. Interpreting the Second Amendment has been one of the Supreme Court's most difficult challenges.

For most of U.S. history, other issues have overshadowed the debate over gun rights. When this debate *has* been front-page news, it stirs up enormous passion. It divides the country in a way that goes far beyond the basic question of who should have a gun and who shouldn't. It asks the greater question: Should the rights of each person in this country be protected against the wishes of the majority? Or does each person have a duty to make personal sacrifices for the good of the country? Keep this in mind as you read about these great debates.

1

Is gun control an issue for each state to decide?

From 1800 to 1865, the issues of gun rights rarely entered the national conversation. However, court cases in Kentucky and Arkansas set the stage for future debates about the Second Amendment. In 1822, the court in the Kentucky case decided that bearing arms was an individual right. In 1842, the court in Arkansas found that people could have guns, but each state could regulate their use and ownership. These opposing views marked the start of the first great debates on lethal weapons …

AFFIRMATIVE SIDE

The Constitution ties gun ownership to a state's ability to form its own militia. That automatically gives any state the right to determine its own firearms laws.

The needs of one state are different from the needs of another. That is why states make their own laws. Gun laws should be no exception.

A Culture of Guns

During the 1800s, America's demand for guns grew as quickly as the population did, especially as the country expanded westward. This period saw the start of several successful firearm manufacturers, including Colt and Remington. Competition between the companies sped up advances in technology. Guns became more accurate, more powerful, and more reliable every year.

During the Civil War, the science of gunmaking took another leap forward. Weapons were often created for purposes other than hunting or personal safety. They were made to kill other humans. More than four million guns were either made in the U.S. or imported from Europe during the war. When peace was declared, young men on both sides of the Civil War brought these weapons home with them—along with the knowledge of how to use them.

NEGATIVE SIDE

The right to bear arms is a Constitutional right guaranteed to all Americans. Unless a person is doing something dangerous or illegal with a gun, the state cannot restrict anyone's use or ownership of firearms. To make such laws violates the nation's founding principles.

Many of these former soldiers headed west seeking adventure and fortune. This was the beginning of what Americans called the "Wild West." Daring train and stagecoach robberies, shootouts on streets and in saloons, and battles with Native Americans all became part of popular culture. These types of stories thrilled kids in the East who read about them in **dime novels**. Meanwhile, performers such as Buffalo Bill Cody, Frank Butler, and Annie Oakley brought audiences to their feet at Wild West shows. Even today, we still celebrate Western heroes and villains in movies, books, and television shows.

This illustration shows Buffalo Bill Cody, one of the heroes of the Wild West.

Denying Gun Ownership

It was in this atmosphere that the first serious questions about gun control reached the Supreme Court. Prior to the Civil War, no one believed strongly that a citizen of the United States should be denied the right to own a lethal weapon. This view changed after the Fourteenth Amendment passed in 1868. It stated that anyone born in the U.S. was now considered a citizen—including millions of slaves freed as a result of the Union's victory over the Confederate Army.

The thought of former slaves suddenly armed sent waves of panic through the South. Laws were passed to keep guns out of the hands of African Americans. Some outlawed people of color from owning all types of guns except for the most expensive pistols. This had the desired effect, as most African Americans in the South could not afford these weapons.

In 1873, after a disputed election in Colfax, Louisiana, a group of whites attacked a group of former slaves gathered at the city's courthouse. More than 100 African Americans were killed, most after they had surrendered. Two members of the white mob were arrested and charged under the Enforcement Act of 1870. The local court decided they were guilty of breaking this federal law, which made it illegal for two or more people to deprive anyone of their constitutional rights, including the right to bear arms. The Supreme Court eventually heard the case (*United States v. Cruikshank*) and overturned the conviction of the two men. The justices said that the Second Amendment allowed states to do as they pleased on the subject of gun rights.

Make Your Case

"No state shall make or enforce any law which shall **abridge** the privileges or **immunities** of citizens of the United States."

▶ *Nathan Clifford, 1876*

Clifford was a Supreme Court justice. He felt that the right of states to make their own laws ended when they limited rights guaranteed by federal laws. In *United States v. Cruikshank*, he was voted down by his fellow justices.

Should states be able to make laws that limit rights guaranteed by the Constitution?

Thirteen years later, the Supreme Court confirmed this position when it upheld the conviction of Herman Presser, who led an armed group of German Americans in Chicago. The group was formed to protect workers against the thugs hired by large companies to break up labor protests. The justices agreed that states and cities could make their own gun laws. However, they warned that a state could not disarm its citizens to the point where they no longer could form a militia.

By 1911, the question of whether a state could make its own firearms laws seemed to have been settled once and for all. In that year, New York enacted the Sullivan Law. It said that everyone owning or buying a handgun had to apply for a police permit.

Now consider *this* ...

The Sullivan Law passed with almost no opposition. Only the National Rifle Association (NRA) objected. The NRA was formed in 1871 to promote rifle ownership, marksmanship, and firearms safety. In 1911, it lacked the experience and organization to oppose New York's handgun law. That would change over the next 100 years. *Should a group that mainly promoted rifles have been concerned with limiting the ownership of handguns in 1911?*

2 Should the government outlaw certain types of weapons?

The Sullivan Law took a new step in the gun rights debate by targeting the owners of handguns because of how these weapons were used. In crowded cities such as turn-of-the-century New York, handguns were often the weapons of choice for criminals. The Sullivan Law tried to address this problem. If each handgun owner had a license on file with the police, fewer of these weapons would fall into the hands of criminals. This attempt to prevent crime by outlawing certain types of weapons triggered the next great debate on lethal weapons …

AFFIRMATIVE SIDE

If it is harder for criminals to obtain lethal weapons, they will be less likely to commit crimes. If a known criminal applies for a gun license, law enforcement will reject the application. If criminals obtain weapons without a license—and are found carrying them— then they will be arrested before a crime is committed.

The First National Gun Control Law

Just as the NRA and other early opponents of gun control feared, the Sullivan Law was used by the New York City Police Department to keep citizens from obtaining handguns. Business owners and people who handled a lot of cash were granted licenses for handguns. So were the wealthy and influential. This method of gun control spread to other states, with varying success.

One way of buying guns without a license was ordering them through the mail. This form of purchase enabled a person to build up an arsenal of weapons without ever applying for a license. Even where licenses were not required, it meant that gun owners could protect their privacy.

In the 1920s, during the early years of **Prohibition**, the use of guns became more widespread. The government had made it illegal to make, move, or sell liquor, but Americans still wanted to buy and drink alcohol.

NEGATIVE SIDE

Criminals will always find a way to get guns, even if they have to do so illegally. But making it difficult for law-abiding citizens to arm themselves could put them in danger. Plus, isn't it a violation of the Second Amendment to prevent any U.S. citizen from obtaining a gun?

They were willing to pay a high price to do so. Criminals saw an opportunity to make a lot of money and formed organized gangs to meet this demand.

Gangsters found it easy to buy their guns through the mail. Once they were armed, they fought each other for control of towns and neighborhoods. Many innocent people were injured or killed in these battles. In 1927, under great public pressure, Congress passed a law banning the mail-order sale of handguns. This marked the first national gun control law.

The "Tommy" Gun

More lethal than the handgun was the automatic weapon. An automatic weapon is one that fires multiple shots

Actor Charles Bronson poses with a Tommy Gun in a photo from the 1958 movie *Machine Gun Kelly*. The film told the story of a real-life gangster from the 1920s and 1930s.

with one squeeze of the trigger. During the 1920s, the Thompson Submachine Gun—or "Tommy Gun"—was the automatic weapon of choice for gangsters, as well as the police and other law enforcement groups. It was loud and powerful, and sprayed bullets over a wide area.

In 1932, Americans elected Franklin Roosevelt as their president. As governor of New York, Roosevelt had fought an attempt to get rid of the Sullivan Law. He also believed that the Tommy Gun should be outlawed. In 1934, Roosevelt pushed through the National Firearms Act. It

Make Your Case

"We cannot say that the Second Amendment guarantees the right to keep and bear such an instrument."

▶ *James McReynolds, 1939*

Supreme Court justice McReynolds was part of a unanimous decision in the case of *United States v. Miller.* The court ruled that a sawed-off shotgun was not protected by the Constitution under the Second Amendment. It was not a typical defensive weapon, nor was it something that would be used by the military.

Why was it important to ban weapons that were altered to be easily concealed, as opposed to easily concealed weapons such as handguns?

placed strict regulations on "gangster weapons," including machine-guns, sawed-off rifles, and shotguns that could be easily hidden under a coat. It also outlawed silencers. A silencer is a metal cylinder that muffles the noise a gun makes.

Originally, Roosevelt hoped to include handguns in the National Firearms Act. However, the NRA worked with gun manufacturers to eliminate them from the bill. Gun rights supporters convinced lawmakers that limiting the sale of handguns would not keep them away from criminals, and that it might leave millions of people defenseless.

In 1937, the **Justice Department** urged the government to reconsider its position on handguns. A year later, the Federal Firearms Act became a law. It made buying and owning handguns a bit more difficult, but the changes were mostly symbolic. The original language of the bill was weakened due to a compromise. A competing law had been proposed with strong support from the NRA. As the organization grew in size and power, it enjoyed more influence in the gun rights debate.

Now consider *this* ...

During the debate over new federal firearms laws, the NRA suggested the creation of a waiting period for buying certain guns. Today, a brief waiting period would give the government time to run a computerized background check on a gun buyer. However, in the 1930s, there were no computers. The idea back then was to give angry people time to "cool off" in case they were buying a weapon to harm or threaten someone else. *Was this "cooling off" strategy reason enough to justify a waiting period?*

3 Do all Americans have the right to bear arms?

Following the passage of national firearms laws in the 1920s and 1930s, the debate over gun rights in America went through a quiet period that lasted a quarter-century. The debate was reignited in the 1960s, when gun violence returned to the headlines. The federal government responded by enacting strong new laws to limit who could purchase and carry firearms. Some of these laws seemed to be aimed at specific groups that were considered especially dangerous. This led to a brand new debate …

AFFIRMATIVE SIDE

The first gun control laws were aimed at gangsters, so it is okay to make new laws targeting other groups that could be violent or dangerous—whether it's people with mental illnesses or organizations that encourage members to carry weapons. It is a matter of public safety.

As this 1960s photo shows, Bobby Seale and Huey Newton believed that carrying a gun ensured their safety.

Surprise at the Statehouse

In the spring of 1967, a group of 30 African Americans walked into the California Statehouse in Sacramento. They hoped to stop the passage of a law they believed was aimed at them. The law would prevent people from carrying a loaded weapon in any California city.

In this era of public protest, it was not unusual for large groups to stage public rallies. However, this was different. The protesters were members of the **Black Panther Party**, and they were armed. Their leaders, Bobby Seale and Huey Newton, believed that the **Civil Rights movement** of the 1950s and 1960s was failing.

NEGATIVE SIDE

Once one group of people is prevented from owning guns, where do you stop? Unless someone is a violent criminal, it is impossible to predict what anyone will do with a gun. If a person or group needs weapons for protection, that's a matter of public safety, too.

"There is no reason why, on the street today, a citizen should be carrying loaded weapons. It is a ridiculous way to solve problems that have to be solved among people of good will."

▶ *Ronald Reagan, 1968*

Reagan was the Governor of California in 1968. He backed the Mulford Act, which barred Californians from carrying loaded guns on their body or in their cars. Opponents of the law claimed it violated their Second Amendment right to defend themselves.

Should citizens be allowed to carry guns to defend themselves outside the home?

The Black Panthers felt that African Americans were being unfairly targeted by police. Seale and Newton urged their followers to take advantage of the Second Amendment and arm themselves for their own protection. Seale had faced off with police before and always felt emboldened when they backed down. But politicians saw the issue differently. They passed the proposed law, thanks in part to the strong support of the California Governor Ronald Reagan.

Civil rights leader Martin Luther King Jr. was assassinated in 1968. His murder provided motivation for Congress to pass gun control legislation.

The Gun Control Act of 1968

Also in 1967, riots broke out in Detroit, Michigan, and Newark, New Jersey. Americans worried that violence might erupt in other cities. Things got worse in 1968 when two prominent political leaders—Martin Luther King Jr. and Robert Kennedy—were murdered with guns in separate incidents. (Kennedy's brother, U.S. President John Kennedy, had been killed by a sniper's bullet in 1963.) All three men stood for peace, justice, and equality. The nation wondered when the violence would end.

Congress soon passed the first nationwide gun control law in 30 years. It raised the minimum age of handgun owners from 18 to 21. It also started a national gun licensing system. Gun control supporters praised the actions of the federal government.

A few months later, the new law was expanded further into what was called the Gun Control Act of 1968. It attacked the problem of gun violence in several steps. The most important focused on who could legally own a lethal weapon. The law made it illegal for anyone to sell a gun to:

1 a person convicted of a **felony** (or on trial for one)
2 a fugitive from justice
3 a known drug addict
4 someone who had been found by a court to be mentally impaired

5 an illegal immigrant
6 someone who had been **dishonorably discharged** from the military
7 anyone under a **restraining order**
8 anyone who had been convicted of **domestic violence**

Although the **legislation** did not discriminate against specific ethnic groups or dangerous organizations, it did spell out clearly who could and could not own a gun in America. Still, many critics claimed this part of the Gun Control Act of 1968 was aimed at the urban poor, and specifically African Americans.

Now consider *this* ...

The Gun Control Act of 1968 did more than criminalize gun ownership for certain individuals. **Provisions** were also written to stop the flow of cheap handguns into U.S. cities. These weapons were called "Saturday Night Specials," and most were made overseas. This part of the law was not successful. Although foreign companies could no longer ship Saturday Night Specials into the country, American firearms manufacturers were still allowed to make them. *What might the government's goals have been in trying to protect American-made Saturday Night Specials?*

4 Are background checks an invasion of privacy?

For the last few decades, almost everyone who wanted to buy a gun from a licensed supplier in America had to undergo a background check. Today, the Federal Bureau of Investigation (FBI) keeps files on people it does not want to purchase weapons. Detailed background checks are commonly done on people who are applying for jobs or loans. However, they are rarely done for any other type of purchase. In an age when personal information is sometimes used to discriminate against someone or steal their identity, there is a new debate ...

AFFIRMATIVE SIDE

A background check is the best way to keep guns out of the hands of people who cannot buy them legally. It lets them know that they cannot walk into a gun shop and walk out with a lethal weapon.

The Brady Act

In 1981, President Ronald Reagan survived an assassination attempt in Washington, D.C. Also wounded were a Secret Service agent, a Washington police officer, and Reagan's **Press Secretary**, James Brady. Brady's wound was the most serious. He suffered a brain injury that left him paralyzed for the rest of his life.

The gunman, John Hinckley, Jr., had purchased his weapon in Texas in 1980 using an old driver's license and a fake address. He had also been under the care of a psychiatrist. Four days before the shooting, Hinckley had been arrested (and then released) at an airport for trying to take three guns onto a plane. As these facts emerged, it became clear that a basic background check might have prevented Hinckley from committing his crime.

This angered Brady's wife, Sarah. She soon became a leader in the American gun control movement.

NEGATIVE SIDE

Gun dealers should not do background checks. They have no right to access sensitive personal information. The whole process is pointless because it is still easy to buy a gun without a background check.

James Brady watches as President Bill Clinton signs the
Brady Handgun Violence Prevention Act in 1993.

In 1987, she helped introduce a gun control law to Congress. It called for a mandatory background check and waiting period before a gun could be purchased. The NRA opposed these ideas, even though the organization itself had once proposed a waiting period. After much debate, the Brady Handgun Violence Prevention Act became a law in 1993.

Make Your Case

"In most states, it's harder to get a job at McDonald's than it is a gun. The American people would be willing to put up with a little more red tape if it stops some of the yellow crime-scene tape."

▶ *Paul Helmke (center), 2007*

Helmke was the President of the Brady Center to Prevent Gun Violence from 2006 to 2011. As he pointed out, a job application asks for more personal information than most forms used for background checks.

How much personal information is "too much" for someone to give before buying a gun?

The Battle Continues

The NRA immediately tried to strike down the Brady Act, claiming that the legislation was unconstitutional. The organization argued that the federal government could not tell state and local police that they had to conduct background checks. The NRA cited the Tenth

"The impression you get is that gun shows, they're just people buying guns and there are no background checks needed. That's not true. Over 90 percent of the firearms sold at gun shows are sold by licensed dealers. Everybody who buys those firearms has to undergo a background check."

► *David Keene, 2013*

Keene was President of the NRA from 1984 to 2013. He believed it would be impossible to have "universal" background checks. For example, he asked how the government planned to do background checks on someone selling (or giving) a gun to a relative.

Should background checks cover the sale of a gun from a person to a spouse or adult relative?

Amendment, which says that states should keep their freedom and independence in matters not covered by the Constitution.

The Supreme Court agreed with the NRA on this point but refused to strike down the Brady Act. Instead, the justices decided that officials could continue with background checks if they wanted to. Only one state halted background checks. In 1998, the federal government took more decisive action when it went online with the National Instant Criminal Background Check System (NICS). Using the phone or a computer, NICS made background checks instantaneous for more than 90 percent of gun purchases from licensed dealers. Since then, more than 2 million purchases have been blocked by NICS. Around two-thirds of the people denied were either convicted felons or fugitives from justice.

Now consider *this* ...

For the most part, the Brady Act does not cover firearms bought at gun shows, over the Internet, sold privately, or given as gifts. That means the felons and fugitives identified by NICS might still be able to purchase guns. Also, the Brady Act only works "one-way"—it does not enable the government to record what guns people are buying. As a result, there is no **national gun registry**, which is a goal of many gun control supporters. Preventing the creation of a gun registry is a major goal of the NRA, which believes that the government intrudes on the privacy of citizens when it seeks this information. *Should the government have the right to keep track of every gun and every gun owner?*

5 Do gun companies have rights?

A company can be held legally responsible if it makes a product that harms or kills people. It can even be forced to change the way it does business. But when firearms manufacturers make a product that harms or kills people, they are not held responsible unless the gun in question has a flaw or defect. If a gun is misused, the fault lies with the person pulling the trigger. Supporters of gun controls insist that gunmakers must do more to protect the public. This has brought the debate on gun rights to the front door of manufacturers …

AFFIRMATIVE SIDE

Guns designed for the military and law enforcement have one purpose—to seriously hurt or kill people. If gun companies sell those weapons to private citizens, and the guns are used to shoot other citizens, then the gun companies should be held responsible.

Gun Control on a Roll

One year after passage of the Brady Act, Congress gave gun control supporters another victory when it passed the Federal Assault Weapons Ban in 1994. "Assault weapon" is a general term used to describe semi-automatic firearms that are made to look like military-style weapons. These types of guns can fire bullets as quickly as someone can pull the trigger, so they have tremendous killing power.

The Federal Assault Weapons Ban was enacted for a period of 10 years. During that time, it was illegal for companies to make or sell this type of weapon. Assault weapons made before 1994 could still be purchased at guns shows and from private collectors. These guns became very popular and very expensive.

Encouraged by their victories—and seeing successful lawsuits against tobacco companies—gun control supporters began suing firearms manufacturers in the late 1990s. They felt the gun industry should pay for the cost of gun violence in America.

NEGATIVE SIDE

Gun makers cannot be held responsible for injuries and deaths caused by their products. People have the right to buy and use military-style weapons—for hunting, target practice, or self-defense—as long as the government says they are legal.

Make Your Case

"Should those whose actions lead to the death or injury of a child get a free pass?"

▶ *Frank Lautenberg (center), 2005*

In 2005, the U.S. Senate voted to shield people and companies that sell firearms from any responsibility for crimes committed with their guns. New Jersey Senator Lautenberg believed the new law should at least include a special rule for families, giving them the right to sue if their children were harmed or killed by someone who should not have been sold a gun. This idea was voted down.

What might the effect have been had this rule been included in the law?

Enter the NRA

For more than a century, the NRA had helped gun companies, but these efforts were rarely coordinated. In 1999, the organization began working hand-in-hand with gun manufacturers to overturn local and state gun control laws. The NRA also pressured lawmakers to draw up bills that would prevent gun manufacturers from being sued.

Not all of the gun companies were on board. For example, Smith & Wesson thought it would be better to work with the government to make guns safer. This angered the

The shootings at Columbine High School in Colorado refocused the gun rights debate for many Americans.

NRA, which organized a **boycott** among its members against Smith & Wesson. This move had its desired effect. The company's sales soon dropped. A short time later, Smith & Wesson pulled out of negotiations with the federal government and agreed to work with the NRA.

The NRA wielded great power over politicians. Lawmakers supporting gun control laws could expect the organization to rally its members to oppose them in elections. The NRA could also use its influence to stop gun control legislation. This became apparent in 1999 after a mass shooting in Columbine, Colorado. Two teenagers purchased weapons at a gun show and then murdered 12 students and a teacher. Under the Brady Act, these types of purchases were not subject to background checks. The U.S. Senate moved quickly to draft a law to close the "gun show loophole." But the NRA convinced enough lawmakers to vote against the legislation, and it was defeated.

Gun Policy in the 21st Century

In 2000, George W. Bush and Al Gore faced off in the closest U.S. presidential election in the nation's history. Bush supported the rights of gun owners. Gore favored gun control measures. The NRA funneled huge amounts of money into the Bush campaign. He won the election by the narrowest of margins, thanks in part to the NRA's support.

Under the Bush administration, the Justice Department took the view that the Second Amendment guaranteed citizens the right to bear arms. In 2004, the Federal Assault Weapons Ban expired. Gun enthusiasts rushed to buy these now-legal weapons, and gun manufacturers offered accessories to go with them. Assault weapons soon became the most profitable products for gun companies.

In 2008, the Supreme Court issued a decision that said a person's right to possess a firearm had nothing to do with service in a militia. It also stated that people had a right to use a gun for lawful purposes, such as self-defense within the home. In another case, the Supreme Court ruled that this right extended to residents of every state.

In the years since Columbine, more mass shootings have occurred. On December 14, 2012, a disturbed 20-year-old forced his way into an elementary school in Connecticut and killed 26 students and teachers. Perhaps because the children were very young—mostly 6 and 7—politicians were less timid this time when it came to debating new gun control laws. But they still faced great opposition.

Now consider *this* ...

With the right to bear arms comes responsibility. Gun owners accept the fact that they are responsible for using their weapons legally and intelligently. They are also responsible for storing them safely. Where that responsibility ends—and how much say the government has in this question—is likely to fuel the debate on lethal weapons for a long time. *Are there issues within the gun rights debate so controversial that the two sides may never be able to compromise?*

6 Find your voice

I n recent years, three issues have been at the center of the debate on lethal weapons. These are complicated questions that invite many points of view. Much like other issues in this debate, they involve economics, politics, powerful fears, and strong emotions. There is a very good chance that people will be debating these issues throughout your lifetime.

For many Americans, the gun rights debate is a family issue.

Neil Heslin was one of many Sandy Hook parents who testified on Capitol Hill about gun control. His son Jesse died in the tragedy.

1 Can gun violence be reduced through laws?

Gun control supporters believe that the more handguns there are, the greater the chance someone will be shot. They also point to studies that show owners of handguns are at greater risk of being killed by their guns or someone else's. The idea of tracking gun sales worries some gun rights supporters. If all adults carried guns, they say, there would be less gun violence. They also say that gun control laws have not reduced gun violence. They believe that other laws would achieve this. For example, stricter jail sentences would make people think twice before using a gun in a crime.

2 Should every gun sale be recorded?

Gun control supporters want people who sell guns for a living to be more careful about where those guns go. They also would like to reduce the chance of guns being sold to criminals. The idea of tracking gun sales worries some gun rights supporters. They believe that if the government knows where all the guns are, it would make it easier for law enforcement to take guns away. Gun rights supporters are also opposed to universal background checks because they believe this policy would be the first step toward creating a national gun registry.

3 Are our schools safe?

Following the 2012 school shootings in Connecticut, President Barack Obama urged Congress to pass new gun laws. The goals of Obama's program included better background checks, the banning of assault weapons, and greater access to mental health services. All of these changes, he said, would make our schools safer. Gun rights groups, including the NRA, opposed these measures. The NRA urged schools to hire armed security guards as a way to make their hallways and classrooms safer.

A month after the Sandy Hook tragedy, President Barack Obama signed an Executive Order for gun control legislation.

All the issues in this chapter are being discussed right now as part of the national gun control debate. Will we ever reach a "middle ground" on the question of lethal weapons? Now is the time to join the national conversation. Think about these issues and consider both sides of these debates. Where do you stand? One day soon—through the candidates you support, through the dollars you spend, and your own personal feelings about firearms—you will have a voice!

7 Point — Counterpoint

America's policy on guns has been greatly influenced by public opinion over the years. That opinion is shaped by many factors, including personal experience, common sense, and what others write or have to say. Just as the way Americans receive information has changed, so has the way we form an opinion. We think about the different sides of an issue. We look at how it affects us, family members, and friends. We consider the best solutions. And we weigh what the smartest and most influential people believe.

This was true in the 1700s and 1800s, when Americans got their information from pamphlets, newspapers, and speeches. It was true in the 1900s, when radio and television brought ideas to an even wider audience. It remains true today, as we scan websites, blogs, and social media. The voices in this chapter have helped shape the debate on gun rights. The words may be a little different, but the passion behind them would fit in any era …

"There has never been a time in my life when I felt that I could take a gun and shoot down a fellow being."
Dwight Lyman Moody, 1899 ◀

"I would like to see every woman know how to handle [firearms] as naturally as they know how to handle babies."
▶ *Annie Oakley (right), circa 1888*

Oakley was a major celebrity in the late 1800s. She taught more than 15,000 women how to shoot during her lifetime. Oakley believed that guns were important for self-defense, and that hunting and shooting were good exercise. Moody, an author and lecturer, was one of the few anti-gun voices in America during the 1800s. He was a member of the Quakers, a religious movement that preaches non-violence. The Quakers believed that settlers could live peacefully with Native Americans by making treaties and working together.

What might America look like today had more people agreed with the Quakers' views?

"The key to effective crime control remains, in my judgment, effective gun control. And those of us who are really concerned about crime just must—somehow, someday—make our voices felt."

Lyndon Johnson (left), 1968 ◀

"The evidence leads one to the conclusion that cheap handguns are considered threatening primarily because minorities and poor whites can afford them."

▶ *William Tonso, 1985*

President Johnson made these remarks before signing the Gun Control Act of 1968. He was disappointed that the law was not stronger. Tonso, a college professor, thought that almost all gun laws start with the idea of disarming certain types of people. He felt this was an obvious form of discrimination.

Is legislation that limits the use of guns a form of discrimination?

"I don't think that the solution to safety in schools is … an armed guard." *Chris Christie, 2012* ◄

"The only thing that stops a bad guy with a gun is a good guy with a gun." ► *Wayne LaPierre, 2012*

LaPierre, the NRA's Executive Vice President, made this statement after the Sandy Hook tragedy. He thought more schools should hire armed security officers. New Jersey Governor Christie opposed this idea. For one thing, he said the cost of placing an armed guard at every door of every school in America might be billions of dollars a year.

What are some other effective ways to make our schools safer?

There has never been a better time to make your voice heard. No matter which side of an issue you take, remember that a debate doesn't have to be an argument. If you enjoy proving your point, join your school's debate team. If your school doesn't have one, find a teacher who will serve as coach and get more students involved. If you want to make a real splash, email the people who represent you in government. If they don't listen now, they may hear from you later … in the voting booth!

GLOSSARY

Abridge — Limit or curtail.

Black Panther Party — An organization formed in 1966 to protect and empower African Americans.

Boycott — A refusal to purchase goods or services from a company.

Chain of Possession — An accounting of everyone who has handled a weapon or other items used in a crime.

Civil Rights Movement — The organized effort by African Americans in the 1950s and 1960s to promote fairness and equality under the law.

Dime Novels — Inexpensive books in the 1800s and early 1900s that featured adventure stories.

Dishonorably Discharged — Released from military service for reprehensible conduct.

Domestic Violence — Physical abuse committed by one person against another in a marriage, family, or other relationship where people share a home.

Felony — A serious crime, often involving violence.

Immunities — Protections from the law.

Justice Department — The part of the government that enforces federal laws.

Legislation — A law or group of laws.

Militia — A group of citizens who take up arms in an emergency to help a country's regular military.

National Gun Registry — A tracking system for every firearm and its owner.

Press Secretary — The person who represents the President of the United States to the media.

Prohibition — A period in the 1920s and early 1930s when liquor was illegal in the U.S.

Provisions — Conditions in a legal document.

Restraining Order — Instructions from a judge to prevent someone from committing certain acts or going certain places.

SOURCES

The authors relied on many different sources for their information. Listed below are some of their primary sources:

Shots in the Dark: The Policy, Politics and Symbolism of Gun Control. William J. Vizzard. Rowman & Littlefield, Lanham, MD, 2000.

Gun Control And Gun Rights. Brannon Denning & Rodney Olsen. New York University Press, New York, 2002.

Guns in American Society: An Encyclopedia of History, Politics, Culure, and the Law. Greg Lee Carter, Editor. ABC-CLIO, Santa Barbara, CA, 2002.

RESOURCES

For more information on the subjects covered in this book, consider starting with these books and websites:

Gun Control. No'l Merino, Editor. Greenhaven Press, Farmington Hills, MI, 2012.

Gun Control: Preventing Violence or Crushing Constitutional Rights? Matt Doeden. Twenty-First Century Books, Minneapolis, MN, 2011.

JustFacts.com
www.justfacts.com/guncontrol.asp and
www. justfacts.com/constitution.asp

INDEX

Page numbers in **bold** refer to illustrations.

AUTHORS

GEOFFREY C. HARRISON and **THOMAS F. SCOTT** are educators at the Rumson Country Day School, a K thru 8 school in Rumson, New Jersey. Mr. Harrison is the head of the math department and coordinator of the school's forensics team. Mr. Scott has been teaching upper school history at RCDS for more than 25 years and is head of that department. They enjoy nothing more than a great debate … just ask their students!